Contents

What Creature is That?

Many creatures in stories are mythical. This means that they are not real, and never have been. These strange creatures often have special powers.

For hundreds of years, people have told stories about mythical creatures. Long ago, people made **sculptures** of mythical creatures and put them on buildings.

An ugly stone creature on a building is called a gargoyle.

This sculpture of a winged lion guards the city of Venice in Italy.

Hundreds of years ago, people in England and France made special picture books about mythical creatures. These books were called bestiaries.

Today, mythical creatures appear in stories, films and games.

Giants and Trolls

Giants

Giants look like people, but they are much bigger and stronger.

Hagrid, in the *Harry Potter* stories, is a half-giant.

In stories, the hero often defeats the giant by being clever. In the fairytale *Jack and the Beanstalk*, the giant is cruel and stupid.

In *Jack and the Beanstalk*, Jack climbs the beanstalk to the giant's castle. The giant tries to kill Jack, but Jack cleverly escapes.

A one-eyed giant is called a Cyclops.

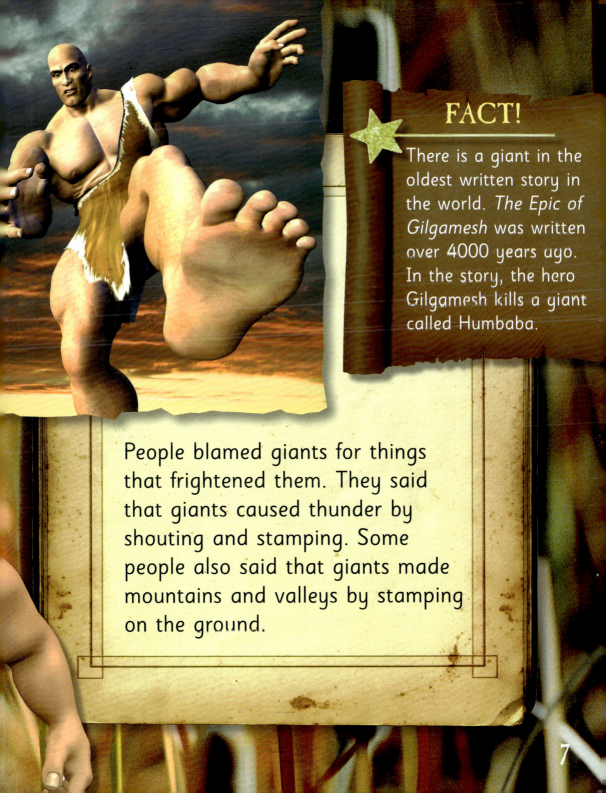

There is a giant in the oldest written story in the world. *The Epic of Gilgamesh* was written over 4000 years ago. In the story, the hero Gilgamesh kills a giant called Humbaba.

People blamed giants for things that frightened them. They said that giants caused thunder by shouting and stamping. Some people also said that giants made mountains and valleys by stamping on the ground.

Trolls

Trolls can be big or small.

Large trolls usually live alone in mountain caves. They have bad tempers and keep to themselves. The grumpy troll in *The Three Billy Goats Gruff* lived alone under a bridge.

Trolls often have big ears and noses.

Small trolls also have bad tempers, but they often live in groups.

Tove Jansson
with models of
the Moomins.

But not all trolls
are grumpy. Tove
Jansson wrote
about a family
of trolls called
the Moomins. The Moomins
are happy and friendly
creatures, and they love
adventures.

Mythical Animals

Many mythical creatures can fly.

Griffins

A griffin has the head, wings and claws of an eagle, and the body of a lion. It has large, pointed ears, which help it to hear very well.

In stories, griffins often guard treasure. Some people say that griffins lay eggs of pure agate in nests of gold.

This statue of a griffin comes from an ancient city in Iran.

There is a picture of a griffin on this shield.

This Chinese dragon has no wings.

Dragons

Most dragons can fly. Many dragons can breathe out fire, but some breathe out mist instead. If you try to kill a dragon by cutting off its head, beware! Some dragons can grow more heads if one is cut off.

Wales has a dragon on its flag.

11

Phoenix

A phoenix is a beautiful, mythical bird of many colours. It can live for more than 500 years.

At the end of its life, a phoenix builds a nest of twigs. The sun starts a fire in the nest. The phoenix dies in the fire, but a new bird rises from the ashes.

This phoenix is on the wall of a Chinese temple.

Basilisks

Some people say basilisks are huge mythical lizards. Other people say they are giant snakes. There are even some people who say a basilisk is an enormous chicken with a snake's tail!

A legend says that you will die at once if you look at a basilisk's eyes.

There is also a type of real lizard called a basilisk.

13

Unicorns

A unicorn looks like a horse. Some unicorns have a beard like a goat. Some have a lion's tail.

All unicorns have a long, twisted horn in the middle of their heads. Unicorn horns are very magical. People used to think that unicorn horns could make a poison safe to drink. In stories, unicorns could make a whole lake or river safe by dipping their horn into the water.

In this Coat of Arms, the lion stands for England. The unicorn stands for Scotland.

FACT!

The unicorn is a symbol of Scotland.

Type of unicorn	Where do they live?	What are they like?	What magic can they do?
earth unicorn	forests and wild areas	kind and wise	They bring good luck. They keep forests healthy.
air unicorn	clouds and rainbows	shy	They can fly and become invisible.
fire unicorn	storms, wild fires and cold places	fierce	They can use spells and potions.
water unicorn	ponds, lakes and seas	proud	They can purify water.

Little People

Elves

The first stories about elves came from Norway, Denmark, Iceland and Sweden. The story of Santa Claus includes elves who make toys in Santa's workshop at the North Pole.

In *The Lord of the Rings* stories, elves have pointed ears and live in forests.

Elves in *The Lord of the Rings* cannot die unless they are killed in battle.

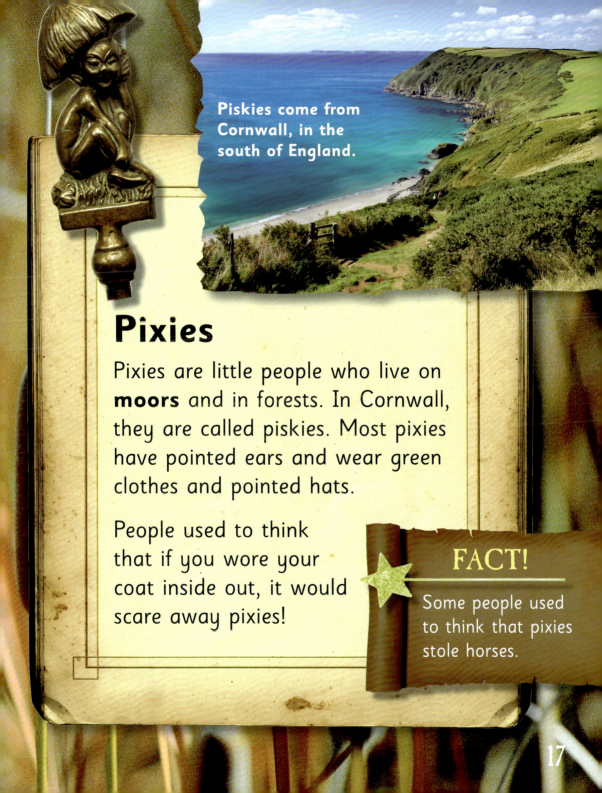

Piskies come from Cornwall, in the south of England.

Pixies

Pixies are little people who live on **moors** and in forests. In Cornwall, they are called piskies. Most pixies have pointed ears and wear green clothes and pointed hats.

People used to think that if you wore your coat inside out, it would scare away pixies!

FACT!

Some people used to think that pixies stole horses.

17

Mythical Creatures of the World

Every country has its own mythical creatures.

Kraken

The kraken is a sea monster from Norway. It is like a giant octopus that attacks ships.

Real giant squid may have caused the legend of the kraken. Giant squid can grow longer than 10 metres, and they are sometimes caught by fishing boats.

This kraken is trying to sink a ship.

In 1847 a strange skull was shown at the Australian Museum. People thought the skull came from a bunyip, but later they found out that it came from a horse.

Bunyip

A bunyip is a water monster from Australian **Aboriginal** stories.

Bunyips live in swamps, rivers and **billabongs**. No one knows what they look like. They may have a tail like a horse and flippers like a walrus.

Tengu

A tengu is half human and half bird. It hatches out of an egg, and lives in the mountains and forests of Japan.

Tengus have wings and a long nose. They can speak without moving their lips.

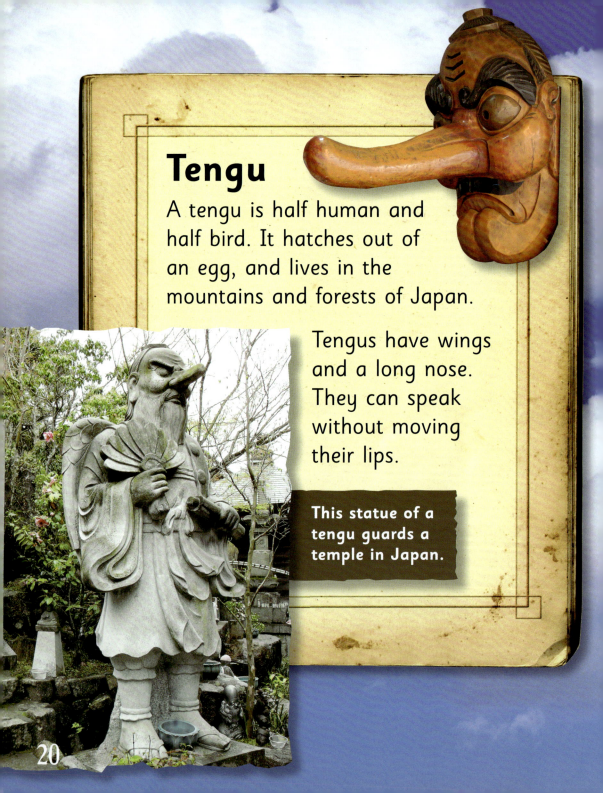

This statue of a tengu guards a temple in Japan.

Bigfoot

Some people in America and Canada say that they have seen a creature called Bigfoot.

It is up to three metres tall and covered in hair.

In 1967, two men filmed what they thought was a Bigfoot. People still argue about whether the film shows a real Bigfoot or a man in an ape suit.

FACT

The Native American name for Bigfoot is sasquatch.

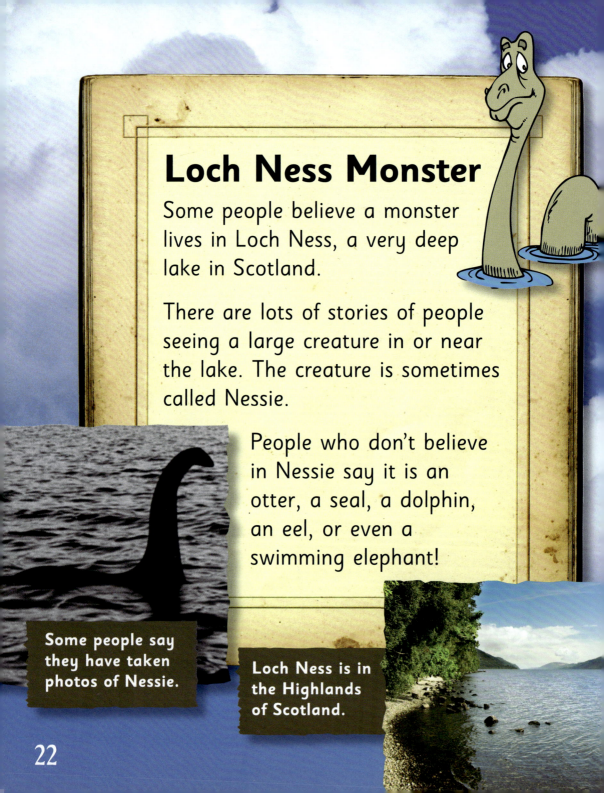

Loch Ness Monster

Some people believe a monster lives in Loch Ness, a very deep lake in Scotland.

There are lots of stories of people seeing a large creature in or near the lake. The creature is sometimes called Nessie.

People who don't believe in Nessie say it is an otter, a seal, a dolphin, an eel, or even a swimming elephant!

Some people say they have taken photos of Nessie.

Loch Ness is in the Highlands of Scotland.

There are many statues of Ku in Hawaii.

Ku

Ku is a Hawaiian god who visited people as a man or dog.

He ate many people, so some men killed Ku with spears and clubs. They cut him into two pieces which were turned into stone.

Glossary

Aboriginal   the first people to live in Australia

agate   a colourful stone

billabongs   Australian waterholes that fill up during a flood

moors   open hills covered in rough grass

sculptures   pieces of art made by carving or modelling shapes out of wood, stone, metal etc.

Index